Hernando Cortés

A Proud Heritage The Hispanic Library

Hernando Cortés

Conquistador and Empire Builder

R. Conrad Stein

Published in the United States of America by The Child's World®
PO Box 326 • Chanhassen, MN 55317-0326 • 800-599-READ • www.childsworld.com

Acknowledgments
  The Childs World®: Mary Berendes, Publishing Director
  Editorial Directions, Inc.: E. Russell Primm, Editorial Director; Pam Rosenberg, Project Editor;
  Melissa McDaniel, Line Editor; Katie Marsico, Assistant Editor; Matt Messbarger, Editorial
  Assistant; Susan Hindman, Copyeditor; Susan Ashley and Sarah E. De Capua, Proofreaders;
  Chris Simms and Olivia Nellums, Fact Checkers; Timothy Griffin/IndexServ, Indexer; Cian
  Loughlin O'Day and Dawn Friedman, Photo Researchers; Linda S. Koutris, Photo Selector
  Creative Spark: Mary Francis and Rob Court, Design and Page Production
  Cartography by XNR Productions, Inc.

Photos
  Cover: Detail from *Portrait of Hernán Cortés* by M. Se Colane
  Cover photograph: Archivo Iconografico, S.A./Corbis
  Interior photographs: The Art Archive/Dagli Orti: 34; Art Resource, NY/Schalkwijk: 16, 21;
  Art Resource, NY/Werner Forman: 7; Archivo Iconografico, S.A./Corbis: 6, 15; Corbis: 9
  (Paul Almasy), 14, 28 (Sergio Dorantes), 32 (Leonard de Selva), 33 (Jeremy Horner); The
  Granger Collection, New York: 13, 26, 27; North Wind Picture Archives: 10-top and bottom,
  11, 12, 17, 24, 29, 31, 35; Stock Montage, Inc.: 8, 18, 19, 22.

Library of Congress Cataloging-in-Publication Data
  Cataloging-in-Publication data for this title has been applied for and is available from the
  United States Library of Congress.

One Reed, The Year Of The God

Montezuma was a powerful Aztec leader who was troubled by strange signs and visions. He consulted members of his tribe who used magic to predict the future, and they told him the signs meant Montezuma's kingdom would be destroyed.

The Aztec emperor, Montezuma, led a mighty nation. His empire in central Mexico stretched from the Atlantic to the Pacific Oceans. Tall pyramids and gleaming palaces rose in his capital city (now called Mexico City). Montezuma believed he was the most powerful man on earth.

Still, Montezuma was troubled by mysterious signs. A three-headed comet hung in the night sky. A temple caught fire and burned to ashes before firefighters could put out the blaze. In the evenings, people in the capital claimed they heard the weeping voice of a woman. The woman would call out, "Come, my children, come with me."

Worst of all, a legend haunted Montezuma's thoughts. The legend told of a god named Quetzalcóatl (kehts-uhl-kuh-WAH-tl) who once lived with the Aztecs. The god was described

A statue of Quetzalcóatl, the Aztec god who was feared and respected by those who worshiped him.

as having white skin and a beard. A rival god drove Quetzalcóatl out of the Aztec nation. Quetzalcóatl was last seen riding a ship over the ocean to the east. Quetzalcóatl said he would someday return and claim the Aztec Empire as his own. **Astrologers** told Montezuma that the god would come back in the year One Reed on the Aztec calendar. One Reed on the European calendar translated to the year 1519.

Aztecs founded the city of Tenochtitlán on the site of present-day Mexico City. Legend has it that they chose that spot after receiving special instructions from their gods.

In February 1519, the Spaniard Hernando Cortés sailed from Cuba toward Mexico. He had white skin and a beard, and he came from the ocean to the east. The similarities between Quetzalcóatl and Cortés were coincidences. They were mere matters of chance. To Montezuma, however, the similarities were the fulfillment of **prophecy.** The god Quetzalcóatl had returned to Mexico. The mighty Aztec Empire was doomed.

The Making of a Conquistador

Hernando Cortés was born in 1485. He grew up in a Spanish region called Extremadura, which lies near the border with Portugal. Dry and mountainous, Extremadura held Spain's worst farmland. Because it was an impoverished province, many young men there chose to become soldiers. Hernando Cortés's father was an officer in the Spanish cavalry. His mother was a devoutly religious army wife.

The Cortés family was wealthy compared to their Extremadura neighbors. When he was 14, Hernando was sent to a school in the town of Salamanca. He must have been an excellent student because he later mastered complex subjects such as history, law, and Latin. But young Cortés stayed in school only

Cortés was not the only famous Spanish explorer who grew up in Extremadura—conquistadores Francisco Pizarro, Vasco de Balboa, Francisco de Orellana, and Hernando de Soto also came from this region.

In 1469, two Spanish nobles, Prince Ferdinand and Princess Isabella, married. Ferdinand and Isabella tried to make Spain prosperous through trade with other nations. In 1492, Ferdinand and Isabella financed the bold voyage of Christopher Columbus (right)—a sea captain from the city of Genoa, Italy. Columbus believed he could sail to the eastern lands of India by sailing west around the world. Instead, he encountered islands in the Caribbean Sea. Columbus mistakenly called the islands the Indies and the people there Indians. Columbus died 14 years later, never realizing

he had discovered the Americas. His accidental find allowed Spaniards to be the first explorers and conquerors of North and South America.

about two years. If one word could describe the Cortés personality, that word would be ambitious. He hungered for gold and fame.

In 1504, 19-year-old Hernando sailed for the island Spaniards called Hispaniola. Today, that island contains the nations of Haiti and the Dominican Republic. Cortés was destined to be a conquistador, a conqueror. In the 1500s, brave, but often cruel, conquistadors

The gateway to the archives of the University of Salamanca is rich in architectural detail. Cortés attended the university as a young man.

came from Spain to carve out empires in the Americas— the lands they considered the New World.

Cortés was offered a farm on Hispaniola but angrily rejected the offer. He said he had not come to the Americas to work a farm like an ordinary **peasant.** He came to find gold. Cortés took part in the conquest of

Christopher Columbus and his crew arrive at Hispaniola in 1492. Cortés visited the island 12 years later, but Columbus was the explorer who first claimed Hispaniola for Spain.

Cuba in 1511. There he did accept a large land grant, where he raised cattle. He married a woman from a wealthy Spanish family and built one of the finest houses in the Americas. But he never gave up his dreams of acquiring gold and achieving military glory.

In 1519, Cortés led a fleet of 11 ships to a territory previously untouched by the Spaniards. That territory is now known as Mexico. Riding on the ships with Cortés were more than 500 soldiers and 16 horses. On the Mexican coast, this army encountered warriors of the Tabascan Indian tribe. The first battle between Spaniards and Native Americans in Mexico broke out. The Tabascan soldiers were quickly overwhelmed. Never before had they seen horses. They believed the horses and the men riding them were one and the same, a single godlike being. The Tabascans had never even dreamed such weapons as guns existed. Now these roaring "fire sticks" killed warriors at long range.

When the battle ended, Tabascan chiefs presented gifts to their conquerors. Cortés was given a young woman slave named Malinche. He didn't know how valuable Malinche would become to the Spanish. Cortés wanted more; he wanted gifts of gold. The

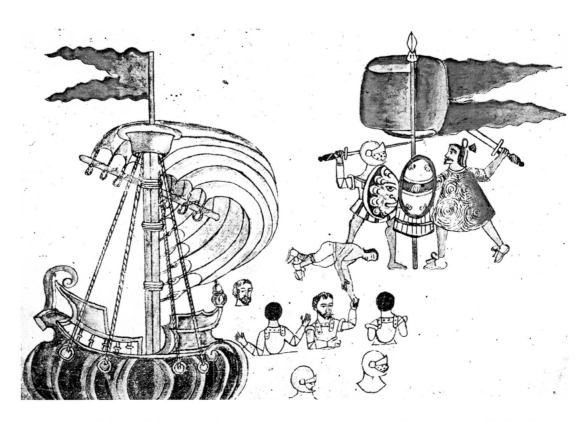

Cortés and his soldiers waded ashore on the coast of Mexico in 1519. The Spanish governor who authorized the voyage canceled it just before Cortés set sail because he was concerned about the cost of the journey and didn't trust the conquistador. Despite the governor's orders, Cortés went ahead with the voyage.

Cortés's every movement on the Mexican coast was being watched and reported to Montezuma. The Aztec capital city was in the mountains, more than 250 miles (402 kilometers) from the coast. Through teams of runners, the Aztecs sent written messages from the coast to the capital in less than 24 hours. The runners were specially trained from the time they were boys. Each runner ran about five miles (8 km) to a post house, where he gave the message to a fresh runner. This track-star telegraph system worked with amazing efficiency.

Tabascans pointed to the mountains that rose to the west. Through sign language, they claimed abundant gold could be found in a great city beyond the mountains. Cortés asked the name of this city. They answered, "Mexico."

Immediately, Cortés made plans to lead his forces across the mountains and seize this **fabulous** city. It would be the first meeting between advanced civilizations from Europe and the Americas. The ambitious conquistador was about to change the world forever.

The Aztecs were amazed by the horses, armor, and guns that Cortés (on horseback) and his men brought to Mexico. Because they feared the Spanish and eventually realized how hard it was to defeat them in battle, the Aztecs tried to please Cortés by offering him gifts.

The March to Mexico

Montezuma sent **emissaries** to meet with Cortés on an island near the coast. The emissaries bore gifts including pieces of gold jewelry. Cortés politely received these presents. In return, he gave Montezuma's agents a Spanish military helmet. Through sign language, he suggested the Aztecs return the helmet filled with gold.

In April 1519, the fleet entered a fine natural·harbor. There Cortés founded the first Spanish town in Mexico. He called the settlement Vera Cruz, meaning "true cross." It is a thriving city to this day. At Vera Cruz, Cortés made a dramatic move. As his men watched in shock, he and a few trusted soldiers set fire to all 11 ships. Why did Cortés destroy his own ships? The commander knew he would face grave dangers on a march to Mexico City. By destroying his fleet, Cortés erased any thought his men might have of retreating to Cuba.

A people called the Totonacs lived near Vera Cruz. One day, Cortés and his followers watched a Totonac religious service. The Spaniards were sickened by what they saw. A slave was placed flat on his back on an altar stone. Four men held the slave.

Cortés and his troops arrive in Vera Cruz. Cortés was concerned that some of his men might desert and ordered that all but one of his ships be destroyed. He reasoned that this would make it harder for any disloyal troops to leave Mexico.

A priest with a sharp knife cut the man's chest open and pulled out his heart. In triumph, the priest held the bloody heart in front of the statue of a god. This was human sacrifice, a common practice among the Indians of Mexico. To the Spaniards, the **grizzly** ritual was proof that the Indian people were savages.

Historians believe some Aztecs may have volunteered to be human sacrifices. Even though it resulted in death, playing this role in the ritual was considered a great honor.

After watching several slaves be killed by the knife, Cortés ordered his men to topple the statue of the Totonac god. Totonac soldiers armed with spears rushed forward to protect their **idol.** Cortés grabbed the Totonac chief. He threatened to kill the chief unless the Totonacs dropped their spears. Reluctantly, the Totonacs agreed. Peace was restored. When Cortés began his march to Mexico City, some 1,000 Totonacs marched with him. The Totonacs had long hated the Aztecs. Totonac soldiers were willing to fight with anyone against their despised enemies.

Spaniards destroy Aztec idols. As Spanish conquistadores claimed land in Central America and South America, European missionaries began the process of trying to convert the natives to Christianity.

Developments in the Totonac nation were reported back to Montezuma. Now Montezuma was certain this stranger from the eastern ocean was no mere man. He was the god Quetzalcóatl, and he had returned to conquer the Aztecs. The legend said that the Quetzalcóatl of old disapproved of human sacrifice. While other Aztec gods demanded bloody hearts, Quetzalcóatl preferred gifts of live butterflies. The stranger's condemnation of human sacrifice stood as further proof of his **divinity.**

Montezuma attempted to make Cortés and his men turn around and go home. He sent agents with gifts of gold. Cortés simply kept the gold and resumed his march. Montezuma planned to ambush the Spaniards at the city of Cholula, some 60 miles (97 km) from the capital. There the slave girl Malinche saved the Spanish army. Malinche possessed the gift of languages. She knew the Aztec tongue and had quickly mastered Spanish. At Cholula, she chatted with local women and learned an Aztec army was poised to attack the Spaniards. She reported this to Cortés. When the attack came, the Spaniards were ready and they easily defeated the Aztec warriors.

After the failed battle at Cholula, Montezuma pondered his next move. He could not bribe the foreigners to go away. He could not defeat them in battle. Now all he could do was wait—wait to meet a god.

The Spanish attack at Cholula was intended to teach the Aztecs a lesson—fighting against Cortés and his troops would not be tolerated. In order to get this point across, the Spanish army killed hundreds of Aztecs and burned many of their temples to the ground.

The Historic Meeting

Coastal people called the Aztec capital Mexico. The Aztec name for the city, however, was Tenochtitlán (tay-noch-tee-TLAHN). Its beginnings were rooted in an old story. It was said that hundreds of years ago, the Aztecs were a homeless people. They roamed the deserts of northern Mexico with nothing to eat but rattlesnakes and insects. Still, the tribe had a plan. Aztec priests said a god ordered them to wander until they saw an eagle perched on a cactus and eating a snake. On that spot they must build a city. In the year 1325, the Aztecs found an eagle sitting on a cactus while devouring a snake. The tribe discovered this magical vision on an island in the middle of a large lake. There they built the city they called Tenochtitlán, meaning "place of the cactus."

Tenochtitlán was the greatest city in the Americas. More than 200,000 people lived there. Tall pyramids

After traveling through jungles and over mountains, the Spaniards were greatly impressed by the beautiful and highly organized Tenochtitlán. Historians believe Tenochtitlán may have had up to 300,000 inhabitants when Cortés arrived. This would have made it one of the largest cities in the world at the time.

rose in the center of the city. Palaces owned by nobles spread out from the pyramid complex. Streets were broad and straight. Canals allowed barges to bring goods to a huge marketplace. Beholding this marvelous capital, an Aztec poet once wrote,

> *The city is spread out in circles of jade*
> *radiating flashes of light like feathers . . .*
> *Beside it the lords are borne in boats,*
> *over them extends a flowery mist.*

Cortés approached the Aztec capital in November 1519. He and his party had marched some 250 (402 km)

At first, Montezuma (left) and Cortés (right) seemed to maintain friendly relations. In reality, Montezuma feared the conquistador and had little choice but to welcome him to Tenochtitlán.

miles from Vera Cruz. The trek had lasted two and a half months. So far, Spanish soldiers had seen little more than mountains and forests. Now the men gazed down at a city so magnificent they thought they were dreaming. One Spaniard wrote, "Great towers and temples and other edifices of lime and stone seemed to rise out of the water. . . . Never before did man see, hear, or dream of anything equal to the spectacle which appeared to our eyes on this day."

Cortés boldly led his army into the capital. Aztecs lined the road, marveling at the horses. Waiting in the city center was Montezuma. The meeting was polite, even friendly. Montezuma gave Cortés several gold

The Sad Night

At the height of the Aztec rebellion, Cortés and the Spaniards found themselves trapped in a city palace. On the night of June 30, 1520, Cortés assembled his men and tried to sneak out of the castle under cover of darkness. The Spaniards were discovered. A wild battle raged on the earthen bridges leading out of the capital. Spanish soldiers jumped into Lake Texcoco and tried to swim to safety. But greed killed them that night. Many Spaniards had stuffed their pockets with gold that they had looted from Tenochtitlán. Weighted down by the gold, many soldiers drowned. Cortés reached the far shore of Lake Texcoco and stood under a tree, weeping over the loss of so many soldiers. In Mexican history, the evening of June 30, 1520, is known as La Noche Triste, "The Sad Night."

pieces delicately carved in the shape of shrimps. Cortés gave the Aztec leader a pearl necklace. Spanish troops were housed in one of the capital's finest palaces. There was peace between the Aztecs and Spaniards.

The peace was short-lived. Less than two weeks after the historic meeting, Cortés seized Montezuma and held him prisoner in his own castle. For six months, Cortés ruled the Aztec nation. The Aztecs, believing Cortés to be a god, obeyed his orders. Finally, the Aztecs learned Cortés was not a divine being. The people rebelled and drove the Spaniards out of their capital. Montezuma was killed in the fighting that swept the city.

The Aztec rebellion in Tenochtitlán occurred after Cortés temporarily left the city. He placed a Spanish officer in charge who was cruel to the Aztecs and drove them to revolt when he massacred several hundred of them.

War and Conquest

Cortés did not accept defeat, even though the Spaniards had been expelled from the Aztec capital. Few military leaders in history possessed his iron-willed determination. More Spaniards arrived at the port city of Vera Cruz. Cortés organized the newcomers into his army. The Spanish leader also gathered Native American allies. The Aztecs were hated by their neighbors because they collected taxes from weaker tribes. Cortés used this hatred to enlist Native American warriors on his side.

Meanwhile, the people of the city of Tenochtitlán were struck by smallpox. One of Cortés's men must have carried the deadly disease to the Aztec capital months earlier. Europeans had lived with smallpox for generations and had acquired some resistance to the sickness. But the people of Mexico had no such resistance. One Aztec account of the smallpox horror read,

"Sores erupted on [the people's] faces, breasts, bellies. They [the infected people] had so many painful sores over their bodies that they could not move. . . . "

With 1,000 Spaniards and about 20,000 Indians, Cortés returned to Tenochtitlán. In June 1521, he launched his main attack. The Aztecs fought bravely for every inch of ground, but many Aztec soldiers had been weakened by smallpox. Those able to fight were slaughtered by Spanish cannons and firearms. Sadly, the marvelous city of Tenochtitlán was almost leveled during the fighting. A Spanish soldier said, "The city looked as if it had been plowed up." The battle for the Aztec capital lasted almost three months. In the end, the brave Aztec army was defeated.

Cortés immediately launched a program to rebuild the Aztec capital. A new city rose on

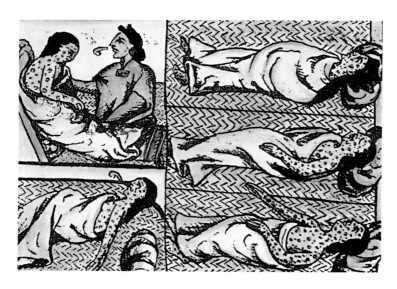

Smallpox had a devastating effect on Mexico's Aztec population. Unfortunately, European explorers would continue to spread smallpox and other diseases to the natives in South America and North America for several hundred years.

Spanish soldiers battle the Aztecs for control of Tenochtitlán in 1521. After overtaking the city, Cortés held the Aztec leader Cuauhtemoc prisoner for four years in the hope of finding out where Aztec treasure was buried. After Cortés finally realized that Cuauhtemoc wouldn't help him, he hanged the Aztec emperor in 1525.

the ashes of the old. Catholic churches replaced Aztec temples. Homes for wealthy Spaniards were built over the ruins of palaces that once belonged to Aztec nobles. The new capital was called Mexico City. It served as the center of Spanish power in Mexico for the next 300 years.

With the conquest of the Aztecs, Cortés established a Spanish empire in Mexico. The empire was called New Spain. Mexico City was its capital. New Spain lasted until the Mexican Revolutionary War of 1810–1821. During that war, Mexican patriots gained independence from Spain.

In the center of modern-day Mexico City is a broad public plaza called the Zocalo. In Aztec times, this plaza was a public market. On the north side of the Zocalo is the National Cathedral. This magnificent church rises on the same spot where an Aztec pyramid once stood. After the conquest of Tenochtitlán, Spanish engineers **dismantled** Aztec structures to make way for new buildings. To this day, some older houses in Mexico City have walls made from huge blocks taken from Aztec pyramids.

Many Aztec buildings were simply buried by Spanish crews. For centuries the ruins remained under the busy streets of Mexico City. Slowly, they reappeared. In the 1970s, workers digging a trench for a telephone cable uncovered the base of an Aztec pyramid. **Archaeologists** carefully cleared the area, and it is now an outdoor museum called Templo Mayor (or "Main Temple"). Also in the 1970s, workers digging a new subway chanced upon a remarkably well-preserved Aztec temple. Engineers built a subway station around the temple. Now, as people wait for the subway train, they can gaze at the beautiful ancient religious building just across the tracks.

The Cortés Legacy

Cortés achieved his dreams in Mexico. He acquired vast holdings of fertile farmland south of Mexico City—25,000 square miles (64,750 square km) of land in all. That is about the size of the U.S. state of West Virginia. On this land, he grew wheat and raised cattle. He also owned gold and silver mines.

The Spanish gained great wealth from their gold and silver mines in the Americas. Unfortunately, Native Americans such as the Aztecs were often enslaved and forced to perform hard labor in these mines.

Cortés became the second-richest Spaniard in the world. Only the king of Spain was richer than Cortés.

Still, Cortés's ambitions knew no limits. He continued to explore and conquer new lands. Cortés led an expedition to the region south of Mexico now known as Honduras. He took another exploring party north to the Gulf of California. The waters

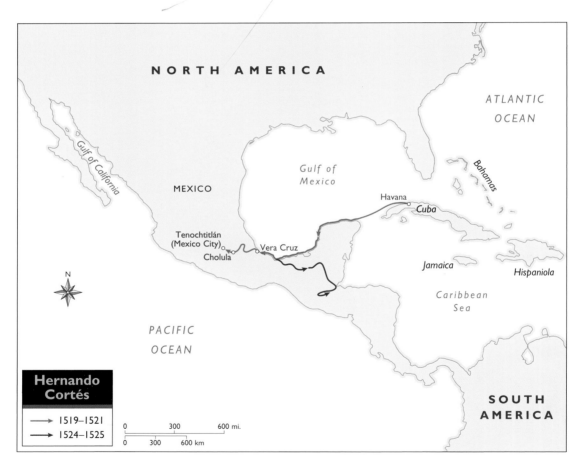

Cortés's desire for wealth in the form of gold and land helped him to establish the Spanish empire in the Americas.

there are sometimes called the Sea of Cortés. He financed these exploring missions with his own money. Although he was fabulously wealthy, he eventually fell into debt.

In 1540, Cortés sailed to Spain. There he appealed to the king to grant him a government job in the Americas. His letters to the king sometimes had the tone of a poor man begging for better treatment: "I thought that having labored in my earlier years I would enjoy rest in my old age." Cortés died on December 2, 1547, in a small town near the Spanish city of Seville. One of his last letters to the king

When Cortés first returned to Spain, he was warmly greeted and received much praise for his voyages to the Americas. As time passed, however, the Spanish king almost completely forgot about Cortés. The aging conquistador found himself having to remind those around him how much he had done for both king and country.

captured the old Cortés pride: "It is better to lose one's wealth than one's soul."

Cortés introduced Spanish civilization to Mexico. His conquest of the Aztecs triggered a mass migration of Spaniards. The migrants brought the Spanish language and the Catholic religion to the Americas. Mexico's lovely villages were built in the Spanish style,

A Spanish husband with his Indian wife and their mestizo child. Mestizo is a term used to describe someone of mixed Spanish and Indian blood.

with a public plaza and a marketplace in the center. The Spaniards also gave Mexico a new race—La Raza. The new race was a mixture of Spanish and Indian bloodlines. Today, about 9 out of 10 Mexicans are mixed-race people, members of La Raza.

In modern-day Mexico, October 12, Columbus Day, is called *Día de La Raza* ("Day of the Race"). It is a joyous holiday when schoolchildren march holding a giant picture of Christopher Columbus. Many villages have a statue of Columbus, and children decorate it with flowers. Columbus is honored because his 1492 voyage led to the establishment of the mixed-race people. Yet Columbus never set foot on Mexican soil. The honor of

A mestizo child holds his toy train. Mestizos make up a large part of the population in Mexico, El Salvador, Honduras, Nicaragua, Colombia, Venezuela, and Chile.

founding La Raza should properly go to Hernando Cortés. But nowhere in Mexico is there a statue of Cortés.

Popular Mexican history brands Cortés as a ruthless conquistador. He came to the Aztec nation as the head of an army. He destroyed the Aztecs in a devastating war. This image of Cortés as a cold and cruel warrior

This statue of Christopher Columbus is located in Mexico City.

Cortés is often associated with the murder and cruel treatment of the Aztecs in Mexico, but it is also important to recognize his intelligence and bravery as an explorer.

masks his accomplishments. He was one of history's greatest explorers and the builder of an empire. Perhaps someday he will be remembered as the complex man who played a key role in the development of modern Mexico.

1325: The Aztecs build Tenochtitlan.

1469: Prince Ferdinand and Princess Isabella, members of Spanish noble families, marry. They plan to make Spain a prosperous and powerful country.

1485: Hernando Cortés is born in the Spanish province of Extremadura.

1492: Ferdinand and Isabella send Italian sea captain Christopher Columbus on a voyage to reach India by sailing west. Columbus discovers islands in the Caribbean Sea and mistakenly calls them the Indies.

1502–1520: Montezuma rules the Aztec Empire of Mexico.

1504: Nineteen-year-old Hernando Cortés sails for Hispaniola, one of the newly discovered islands.

1511: Cortés participates in the Spanish conquest of Cuba.

1519: Commanding a fleet of 11 ships, Cortés sails from Cuba to the unknown lands of Mexico. He founds the city of Vera Cruz on the Mexican coast. Cortés enters the Aztec capital city (today's Mexico City) with soldiers and Indian warriors.

1520: Cortés and his army retreat from the Aztec capital.

MEXICO

1521: Cortés begins a major assault on the Aztec city of Tenochtitlán. The battle for Tenochtitlán ends. The old city is in ruins, and Cortés immediately starts rebuilding. The city built by Cortés over the ruins of Tenochtitlan is called Mexico City. It becomes the capital of New Spain, the Spanish empire in the Americas.

1524: Cortés explores the lands of Honduras to the south of Mexico.

1535: Cortés sails to what is now known as the Gulf of California.

1540: Deep in debt, Cortés returns to Spain to ask the king for an administrative job in the Americas.

1547: Cortés dies in a tiny town near Seville, Spain.

1970s: Workers digging trenches for telephone cables and tunnels for a new subway in Mexico City uncover the ruins of Aztec pyramids and temples.

archaeologists (ark-ee-OL-uh-jists) Archaeologists are scientists who study ancient civilizations. Archaeologists carefully cleared an area of land that is now an outdoor museum called Templo Mayor.

astrologers (uh-STROL-uh-jurz) Astrologers are people who try to predict future events by reading patterns in the stars. Astrologers told Montezuma the god Quetzalcoatl would come back in the year One Reed on the Aztec calendar.

dismantled (diss-MAN-tuhld) Something that is dismantled is taken apart. Spanish engineers dismantled Aztec structures to make way for new buildings.

divinity (duh-VIN-ih-tee) To have divinity is to have a godlike character. Cortés's condemnation of human sacrifice was further proof of his divinity.

emissaries (EM-uh-sar-eez) Emissaries are agents or representatives of another person. On an island near the coast of Mexico, Cortés met emissaries of Montezuma.

fabulous (FAB-yuh-luhss) Something that is fabulous is wonderful or amazing. Cortés made plans to march across the mountains and seize the fabulous Aztec city.

grizzly (GRIZ-lee) Something that is grizzly is bloody or gory. To the Spaniards, the grizzly ritual of human sacrifice was proof the Indians were savages.

idol (EYE-duhl) An idol is a statue or painting worshipped as a god. Totonac soldiers armed with spears protected their idol from the Spaniards.

peasant (PEZ-uhnt) A peasant is a poor farmer who has his own small farm or works on someone else's farm. Cortés claimed he had not come to the Americas to work on a farm like an ordinary peasant.

prophecy (PROF-uh-see) A prophecy is a prediction of future events. To Montezuma, the similarities between Quetzalcóatl and Cortés were the fulfillment of prophecy.

Books

Calvert, Patricia. *Hernando Cortés: Fortune Favored the Bold*. New York: Benchmark Books, 2003.

DeAngelis, Gina. *Hernando Cortés and the Conquest of Mexico*. Philadelphia: Chelsea House, 2000.

Stein, R. Conrad *The Aztec Empire*. Tarrytown, N.Y.: Benchmark Books, 1996.

Tanaka, Shelley, and Greg Ruhl (illustrator). *Lost Temple of the Aztecs: What It Was Like When the Spaniards Invaded Mexico*. New York: Hyperion Press, 1998.

Web Sites

Visit our Web page for lots of links about Hernando Cortés:
http://www.childsworld.com/links.html

Note to parents, teachers, and librarians: We routinely check our Web links to make sure they're safe, active sites—so encourage your readers to check them out!

About the Author

R. Conrad Stein was born in Chicago, Illinois. At age 18, he enlisted in the U.S. Marines and served for three years. He later attended the University of Illinois and earned a degree in history. Mr. Stein is a full-time writer. Over the years, he has published more than 150 books, mostly history and geography titles. The author was especially pleased to write for A Proud Heritage because he lived in Mexico for seven years during the 1970s. The Stein family still spends most of the summer months in the town of San Miguel de Allende in central Mexico. The rest of the year, Mr. Stein lives in Chicago with his wife, children's book author Deborah Kent, and their daughter, Janna.